D1083792

# Our Six-Legged
# FRIENDS and ALLIES

# Our Six-Legged

# FRIENDS and ALLIES

## Ecology in Your Back Yard

by Hilda Simon

*Illustrated by the author*

THE VANGUARD PRESS · NEW YORK

*To Evelyn Shrifte,*
*whose interest and enthusiasm,*
*both as a publisher and as a friend,*
*have proved invaluable to my work.*

# Contents

# List of Illustrations

*See pages 83 and 84 for illustrations showing the actual size of the insects discussed in this book, with the exception of the dragonfly, which is somewhat reduced.

# Introduction

There are thousands of groups of insects in the world—an insect is an animal characterized by having six legs—and most people are indiscriminately afraid of them all. But this attitude is as incorrect as being fearful of none, for many insects are not man's natural enemies but his friends. These are the insects we shall talk about in this book.

These friendly insects belong to widely differing groups and have widely differing living patterns. They do, however, have one thing in common: while in the larval or adult stage, their food consists of other insects. This is the fact that makes their existence so valuable to man, for by preying on insects harmful to man and his crops, they advance human well-being. Some of these beneficial predators show commendable selectivity in their food preferences, living exclusively on several of the most destructive plant-devouring species. For that reason, these predators are considered by some biologists as one of the best and most desirable alternatives to the chemical poisons by which pest insects have been controlled over the past decades. While such poisons often bring instant and absolute, if short-term, results, they also cause widespread and unprecedented damage, adversely affecting countless links in nature's delicately balanced household. The full impact is only now becoming evident. Even the most stubborn advocate of chemical control has had to concede the consequences of indiscriminate use of insecticides as revealed by recent alarming discoveries. These include the finding of dangerously high levels of pesticide residues not only in many human foods but also in the bodies of animals living far from the areas where the poisons were used.

Widespread popular concern for the quality of our natural environment is a very recent development, having assumed broader dimensions only within the past few years. Less than a decade ago, people who advanced many of the predictions made by the late Rachel Carson in her famous book *Silent Spring* were as often as not met with polite disbelief, if not open derision. I well remember an evening at my home when a friendship of long standing was seriously strained over a disagreement about poisonous chemical sprays. My arguments against the use of such pesticides aroused nothing but amused disbelief, culminating in the witty remark: "Who needs bugs?" And only three or four years ago, a well-known television personality interrupted her show to scream, "Look! An insect! Kill it! Kill it!"

These two statements pretty well summed up the attitude—mainly ignorance—of a great many persons towards not just insects but toward wildlife in general: it was considered expendable. Only a relatively small group of naturalists and nature-lovers believed that all animals, including insects, have important and indispensable parts in nature's complex web of life and that man has upset this balance at the risk of his own survival. Such opinions were most often considered the impractical ideas of odd if harmless cranks.

Fortunately, those days are past. My friend who thought insects (and many other animals) expendable has long since joined a wildlife organization and takes an active interest in conservation. The dangers of pesticides have been clearly recognized, and even governments in many countries are beginning to take steps to ban certain poisons. Conservation and ecology have become fashionable. But, while broad popular support in these fields certainly is to be welcomed, there are disquieting signs of environmental concern degenerating into a mere fad, with all the dangers of superficiality and the risk of exploitation by special interests that often accompany such temporary fashions.

This trend is regrettable because it would defeat the very purpose it set out to accomplish. We have to chart programs for the future: saving remaining wildlife refuges, limiting the use of chemicals, preserving oxygen-giving vegetation, and cutting down pollution. These are difficult goals. There are no quick or cheap solutions, no gimmicks or cure-alls. The will to act and the knowledge of what is important are needed for even moderate steps in the right direction. How can chemical fertilizer help kill a lake? What does that do to the immediate environment? Why is it better, and in the long run more economical, to spend $3 on a batch of live ladybirds—commonly known as ladybugs—than $1.50 on a can of aphid-killer? Why should the large dark wasp that builds mud nests under your porch roof not be killed? These and countless others are questions that most persons still cannot answer, despite all the often rather vague talk about the need to protect our environment. While the individual may be unable to do much to protect wildlife in Africa, he can do his part to protect his own back yard and his immediate neighborhood, and the sum total of such vestpocket projects could have a considerable impact on the overall picture.

This is where our younger citizens can perform valuable services. They have the time needed for patient observation and acquisition of pertinent knowledge, time often not available to their parents burdened with the need to make a living. Young people can therefore become important in passing on this information, and would probably enjoy this activity much more than they do many a television program. I find that children normally are fascinated by living things and like to know how they live and what they do. But children today are often sidetracked from learning about such facts by the presentations of many textbooks and biology courses. Because "nature studies" are considered old-fashioned and not "scientific" enough, biology courses are frequently loaded with technical information, such as classification and biochemistry. But learning about classification of animals and classes, suborders and superfamilies and DNA and ATP—while in itself certainly useful and interesting—does not begin to supply the information about the lives and interrelationships of insects and other creatures—information we need if we want to achieve a broad understanding of environmental goals. In this age of space exploration, we should give equal time to the exploration of the microcosm of insects. There are dramas to be witnessed in the grass, on bushes and flowers in any back yard or garden, dramas not only of hunters and hunted and sudden death but also of co-existence and the triumph of survival.

In particular, such studies cannot help but increase understanding of what we hope to achieve by what is called "biological control" of pest insects. For that, some knowledge of the latters' habits is necessary. What exactly constitutes a "pest"? One dictionary definition says simply: "any destructive insect." This, of course, means not one individual insect, but rather a  species whose feeding habits are collectively destructive. Regardless of how much they eat, one or two caterpillars will not be capable of defoliating a tree. By definition, then, injurious insects have to occur in great numbers in order to be destructive. A pest insect therefore is one whose reproductive powers are considerable and that, if not checked, is capable of habitually building up huge populations. Without controls, the offspring of a single leafhopper, a small plant-sucking insect, would number about five hundred million in just one year; among aphids (also known as plant lice), this figure would be many times higher.

It is especially plant pests such as leafhoppers, aphids, and the related scale insects, as well as certain moth and butterfly caterpillars, that form the diet of the insect allies we shall discuss in this book. We shall tour orchards, gardens, and fields to observe trees and other plants on which we can find the tiny "pest patrols" in action. Such observation will demonstrate that in nature the accent is on balance, limitation, and control—not on extermination. In nature's scheme, pest species have as much right to live as do beneficial insects. Under normal conditions, a delicately balanced system of checks and counterchecks makes sure that all get a chance to survive. Those that destroy through overpopulation are controlled by the predators. Thus, the predatory insects act as agents of conservation for many plant groups and are intimately connected with the evolution of the world as we know it. It is fascinating to speculate on what kind of world, with what kind of plant life, would have evolved without the regulating activities of these small, often unseen or ignored, pest patrols. Would man and his culture have been able to develop without them? Merely by raising such questions we can more fully appreciate the importance of the interdependence of all life on earth. If, for the sake of his own survival, man wants to restore the balance of the badly abused natural environment, our insect allies cannot be ignored.

# Dragonflies

One of my fondest childhood memories brings back pictures of a river bank on a midsummer day, with blue skies, white clouds, hot sun, and cool grass underfoot. Near the town where we lived, a stretch of the river not far from a small dam had been converted to permit swimming, with diving boards, a pool for children, and a large meadow of close-cropped grass for sun-bathing. While I enjoyed swimming very much, I did not like to stay long in the sun, being too fair-skinned to tolerate much of it without getting painful burns despite creams and lotions. Thus, I usually took advantage of the time when the others were dozing in the sun after a swim to wander upstream in the shade of the trees that bordered the river. It was quiet there, and the grass was high and cool around my feet. Spotted leopard and bright green grass frogs jumped as I moved, and it was on such a day that I captured a leopard frog. It became a member of our family, so tame that it took food from my fingers and would sit patiently on my shoulder or on the table while I did my homework.

In the water among the tall bulrushes life abounded: there were fish, and tadpoles, and curious creatures that at the time I often could not identify. My favorite spot was a jutting rock where I liked to sit quietly and just watch and listen, especially in the "witching hour" of high noon, when most creatures sought protection from the hot sun, sound and movement all but ceased, and time seemed to stand still. One day, as I idly watched the rather clumsy maneuvering of a heavy-bodied fly a few feet away, a large dragonfly, with glittering wings and the blue-green flash of a slender body, appeared suddenly and silently out of nowhere. Grabbing the fly a mere three feet from my face, it darted off as suddenly as it had come, only to reappear a little later and alight on a dry stalk, where it seemed to be busily wiping its face. I could clearly see the long, heavily net-veined wings, the huge, bulging eyes, and the slender, brightly colored, segmented abdomen. At once startled and fascinated by this close encounter, I had the impression that the dragonfly had returned only to inspect me and was looking me over not out of fear but, instead, with idle curiosity. From that day on, dragonflies—beautiful, unusual, mysterious survivors of a distant past—were included in my group of favorite insects.

For ages, people of many countries have been fascinated by dragonflies. Poets have immortalized them in their songs and stories. Painters and sculptors have pictured these beautiful insects in their works of art, especially in the Orient. Insect folklore in many lands includes stories about dragonflies, some quite fantastic, and the great number of popular names, such as darning needles, snake doctors, mosquito hawks, and so on, reflect the fact that the popular imagination was inspired by these unusual insects. Scientists are not immune to this fascination: in several instances entomologists have continued their childhood interest in dragonflies and developed it into a lifelong study, gaining international reputations as specialists in the subject.

In view of this age-old interest, it is all the more surprising to find that, until a few hundred years ago, no one had the slightest idea how dragonflies develop. Their larvae, which in old texts often were referred to as "water lizards," were believed to be animals completely unrelated to the mature insect. Only relatively recently—about two hundred and fifty years ago—was the connection between the peculiar-looking water monsters and the beautiful, winged dragonflies discovered.

Because dragonflies are not only attractive and unusual, but also valuable predators, they are included in this book. Both as larvae and as adults, they consume large quantities of insects, such as mosquitoes and flies, that are a nuisance (and sometimes a threat) to man and his domestic animals. Entomologists differ on the value of dragonflies as controllers of such insects. Some consider it very slight, others considerable. I lean to the latter view, because I have noticed in several instances a definite connection between the appearance of dragonflies in numbers and the local decrease of mosquito and fly populations. Since I have observed this in different countries, and once as the result of a deliberate test, I consider it safe to state that dragonflies in any given locality will drastically reduce the number of insects such as mosquitoes, flies, and gnats. We shall see later on in this chapter exactly why they are especially efficient as mosquito killers.

Dragonflies and their smaller cousins, the damselflies, are members of the world-wide insect order* Odonata. Numbering more than four thousand species, they are found wherever they have access to fresh water—streams, lakes, ponds, or pools—which they need in order to lay their eggs and for the subsequent development of their larvae, which can live only in water. That does not mean, however, that

*Zoological terms used in this book are explained in the Glossary, p. 89.

dragonflies are not often encountered far from water, for they are powerful fliers and great travelers—in fact, one species is called "the globetrotter." Some even undertake long-distance migrations similar to those made by the well-known monarch butterfly.

The dragonflies of today are closely related to some very ancient forms. Fossil evidence tells us of huge dragonflies with wingspreads of nearly thirty inches that flew and hunted in the primeval world hundreds of millions of years ago. These monsters disappeared before the Age of Dinosaurs. Today, although dragonflies are among the largest of living insects, no species has a wingspread of more than seven inches, and few attain that size. The average dragonfly probably measures between three and four inches across.

In accordance with their ancient lineage, dragonflies are what entomologists call "primitive" insects, meaning that they have retained the features of their ancestors of millions of years ago without any basic change or adaptation. For example, their flight apparatus is positively archaic compared to that of advanced insects such as bees and flies. Because of a special muscle arrangement and other sophisticated anatomical features, a bee can beat its wings several hundred times per second, whereas dragonflies have a wingbeat of only thirty times per second. Nor have dragonflies ever evolved the ability to fold back their wings to lie flat over their bodies—a feature found even in such primitive insects as roaches. Instead, dragonflies hold their wings stiffly outspread in a horizontal position, and damselflies fold them vertically over their backs.

All this may sound as though our "aerial dragons" are poor fliers compared to more advanced insects, but nothing could be further from the truth. Their great agility, strength, and capacity for sustained flight make them masters of the air, capable of capturing insects that have the most highly advanced flight apparatus. With all their archaic features, dragonflies are superbly equipped for their way of life and

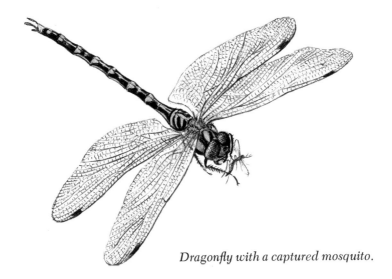

*Dragonfly with a captured mosquito.*

have proved to be a highly successful group, holding their own even in a world so drastically changed by man's manipulations.

A powerful predator, the average dragonfly is a match for almost any flying insect.* Its two pairs of wings are of almost equal length and are supported by a tight network of veins. Such bracing lends them great strength. The head is dominated by the huge bulging compound eyes, which often meet in the front. In the larger species, the eyes may have more than 20,000 individual facets, which give them a greater range of vision than that of a human being. The head, which is hollowed out in the back, can be rotated freely because it is only loosely attached to the prothorax. A dragonfly thus can look in all directions, which makes sneak attacks upon it almost impossible. I know, for I have tried often enough and have succeeded only a few times in catching one by hand. Even so, one of these captures was not an unqualified success: I failed to keep my fingers out of reach of my prisoner's powerful jaws and was nipped badly enough to warrant the exercise of more care during the next attempt. Anyone who has ever tried capturing dragonflies will understand why, in some regions

*See page 87 for a diagram showing the parts of an insect.

of Germany, the expression *"Libellen fangen"* ("catching dragon-flies") is synonymous with attempting the impossible. The smaller damselflies, on the other hand, are relatively easy to capture.

Prey spotted by the dragonfly's keen eyes (which are said to perceive movement up to forty yards away, most unusual for insects) are scooped up by the long, spidery legs, which are equipped with sharp spines. The legs can be used in this way because they are placed well forward on the body through the tilt of the broad thorax, an arrangement providing support for the powerful flight muscles. The wings are located behind the third pair of legs, in marked contrast to those of other insects.

In flight, the foremost and probably also the second pair of legs are held to form a basket with which the prey is captured. Once the victim has been grabbed, the spines exert a vice-like grip as the food is brought up and stuffed into the dragonfly's mouth, which is equipped with sharp jaws. Watching a dragonfly eat an insect is reminiscent of seeing a hungry person gorge himself with the help of both hands.

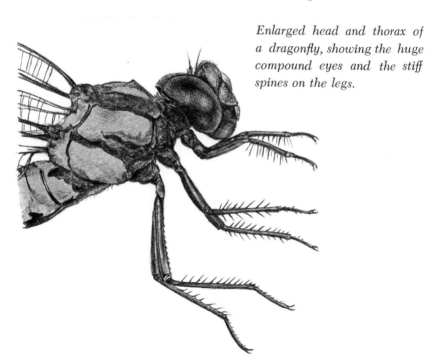

*Enlarged head and thorax of a dragonfly, showing the huge compound eyes and the stiff spines on the legs.*

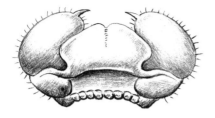

*Lower lip of a dragonfly, modified to form a pincer-like instrument with which prey may be firmly gripped.*

Although a useful tool for capturing prey, the dragonfly's legs have lost most of their original function. Creatures of the air, relying on their wings for locomotion, dragonflies cannot walk on the ground. They can, however, cling to plants and other surfaces on which they alight for a rest, which is sufficient for them.

Observing a dragonfly as it feeds on a swarm of midges or mosquitoes would convince anyone that this insect has a voracious appetite. This holds even more true for the larvae, commonly called nymphs. As mentioned earlier, the larvae live and complete their development in the water, where the eggs are laid by the female shortly after mating. Mating takes place in the air during the so-called tandem flights, when male and female fly together, the male holding the female by the neck with a special pair of abdominal claspers. Many male dragonflies stay with the female while she lays her eggs, hovering above as she dips her body into the water, and the males of some species even lead the females to desirable locations. This is most unusual behavior for insects, and is another of the many interesting features of dragonflies.

Most of the eggs and the young hatchlings wind up in the stomachs of other animals, for the watery world in which the larvae live is filled with predators ranging from other insects to fish. But many survive, grow, and become formidable predators in their own right. No creature that can be overwhelmed is safe from their attack; in fact, the killing of young fish in hatcheries by a few of the larger dragonfly larvae may occasionally present a problem. That, and the habit of hovering around beehives to grab emerging bees (especially among adults of one species), are the exceptions in the otherwise highly beneficial feeding preferences of dragonflies.

*Male and female ruby-spot damselflies. The male is supporting the female while she submerges herself in the water to lay her eggs in the stem of a plant.*

Because dragonfly nymphs often live in the same kind of habitat frequented by mosquito larvae, the latter form a very large part of the immature dragonfly's diet. Mosquitoes are hunted by the same "dragon" in the water and in the air: their young are eaten by the nymphal form, their adults by the transformed, flying insect.

Dragonfly nymphs are peculiar-looking monsters. They superficially resemble huge earwigs, except for their large heads, big eyes, and tiny antennae. They have two unusual and distinctive features. One is a kind of "lazy tongs" arrangement of the lower lip, or labium. This "capture mask" is greatly lengthened and hinged, and it can be withdrawn and folded beneath the face when not in use. Let an unwary prey move close, though, and the mask is shot out with incredible speed to capture and draw back the victim.

The second special feature is an arrangement of gills in the posterior part of the abdomen. This gill chamber can suck in fresh water and, with it, oxygen; by contracting the gill, the nymph expels water and jet-propels itself forward—often out of the reach of danger.

The fact that dragonfly larvae are rapacious creatures can be confirmed by anyone willing to take on the chore of rearing one. I remem-

*A dragonfly nymph, the "water lizard" of old texts, that has just captured a mosquito larva with the help of its "mask".*

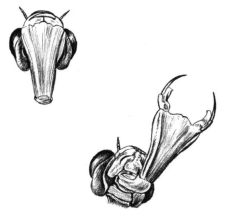

*The "mask" of a dragonfly nymph, shown both folded and extended.*

ber one half-grown nymph that I installed in its own specially prepared aquarium. At first it tried to hide, but very soon it became quite bold, emerging from its hiding place to pick up food whenever I tapped on the glass. At that time, home-owners in our town kept large barrels beneath the gutter spouts of their houses to catch rain. These barrels were ideal breeding places for mosquito larvae—the dragonfly nymphs' favorite food—so I made the rounds of these rain-water barrels every day, scooping up the mosquito larvae in a small net. I did not keep track of the total number I collected in this way, but I do know that all the barrels in the neighborhood were exhausted after a few weeks, and so was I. Fortunately, the nymph was in the final stage of its larval development. Otherwise, I think, I would have given up and returned it to its native pond.

*Mosquito and its larva, a favorite prey of dragon- and damselflies.*

At least one entomologist did keep track of the numbers of insects fed to a dragonfly nymph over the course of the year it took to complete the larval stage. Philip P. Calvert, whose lifelong study of dragonflies has made him one of the outstanding authorities on the subject, found that this one larva consumed some 3,200 insects, most of them mosquito larvae, before changing into an adult.

Duration of the larval stage varies considerably in the different species; it may last from a few months to several years. Finally the time comes for the nymph to end its aquatic existence and change into the winged adult. Crawling up on a reed or twig, it rests quietly until the larval skin splits along the back, and the mature insect, bloated and with crumpled wings, pulls free. After a period—usually a few hours—during which the wings expand and stiffen, the moment arrives: the dragonfly takes off on its maiden flight and begins its airborne existence, far removed from the murky depths of the water in which it grew and developed.

Strange and beautiful, living remnants of the prehistoric past, dragonflies should be valued and protected perhaps as much for their beauty as for their unquestionable value as beneficial predators.

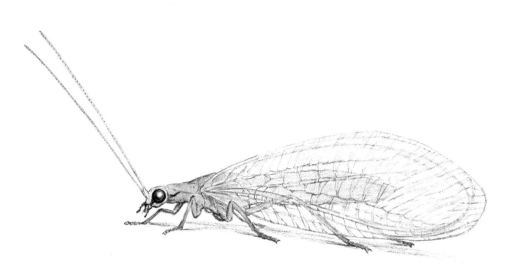

# Lacewings

Among the myriad different insects normally attracted by lighted windows or doors on a summer's night, one can hardly fail to find a few delicate, light-green creatures measuring a little more than half an inch in length. They have filmy, veined wings that they hold, tent-like, over a slender body; long, thin antennae; and prominent red-gold or brass-colored eyes. These insects are members of the family Chrysopidae, a Greek word meaning "golden-eyed," and are popularly known as green lacewings. Both the scientific and popular names are descriptive, for the lacy, veined wings, which extend far beyond the body, are as characteristic of these insects as are their large, metallic, and beautifully iridescent eyes.

Green lacewings are one of the fewer than two dozen families that make up the relatively small order of the Neuroptera, or nerve-winged insects. These include the dobson flies and snake flies, as well as the ant lions. With a few notable exceptions, little is known about the neuropterous insects, or about their development and habits—chiefly because most of the adults are not active by day, and also because they are never really abundant.

Green lacewings are found in many different parts of the world. In North America, about fifty species are known. All of them are very similar, having, as adults, more or less the same habits and, as larvae, the same food preferences. One common European species is found not only over all of Europe but also in Africa.

Nocturnal insects, green lacewings are not often seen by day. After the sun has set and night begins to fall, they become active. Despite the proportionately large size of the wings, their flight is weak and rather clumsy, like that of many neuropterous insects. It is actually more a slow, awkward fluttering, which would make them easy prey for predators during daytime. As it is, they are sometimes caught by bats and night birds such as swifts. Most predators, however, tend to leave them alone after one or two attempts at eating them. Apparently the odor emitted by lacewings is the main reason for this relative immunity: especially when squeezed or otherwise disturbed, these insects secrete an evil-smelling (and presumably also foul-tasting) liquid from two glands located on either side of the first thoracic segment. This reaction has resulted in their local nickname of "stink flies." The odor of the European species is much more pronounced than that of the North American kinds. (I can confirm this from my own experience: as a child, while picking up

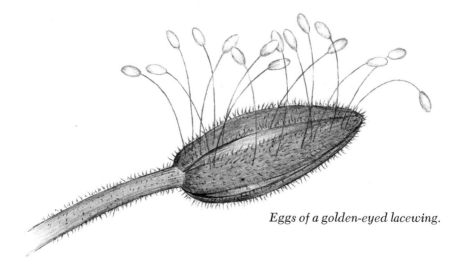

*Eggs of a golden-eyed lacewing.*

*A lacewing larva hatching from an egg.*

and releasing lacewing flies that had accidentally strayed into the house, I often had to fight down nausea as the vile odor attacked my nostrils.) While they are thus relatively free from attacks by large predators, lacewings sometimes suffer from parasites such as mites and sand flies, which ride on their wings and suck blood from the lacewing's veins.

After mating, the female lacewing lays her eggs among the foliage of trees or bushes, or on flowers. She deposits them close to one another in small groups that may number up to a few dozen. Each egg is attached to one end of a long, thin stalk whose other end is fastened to a leaf or a petal. The oval eggs, whitish or greenish, thus look like tiny buds growing from thin delicate stems. It is thought that this method of depositing the eggs serves as a measure of protection against the cannibalistic tendencies of the lacewing larvae. Many entomologists believe that, were the eggs laid side by side, the earlier hatchlings would promptly make a meal of their tardier brothers and sisters. While this apparently has not been proved, it appears to be a plausible theory.

What has been established beyond any doubt is the voracious appetite of the newly hatched lacewing larvae, an appetite that continues unabated throughout their entire larval life. And because their diet consists exclusively of plant pests that infest and seriously injure and sometimes even destroy many of man's most valuable cultivated plants, the lacewing larvae's insatiable appetite is an important aid in checking such pest insects.

Although adult lacewings are also predatory, they eat relatively little compared to their larvae, which, on the other hand, are constantly on the prowl for prey as they crawl about among the vegetation. Despite the fact that they measure only about one quarter of an inch in length, they attack any small, soft-bodied insect they encounter, piercing it with their long, hollow, curved mandibles and sucking their body juices until only the dry skin remains. In this way they attack and decimate many different species of aphids, among them the destructive cabbage, pea, and cotton aphids. In addition, lacewing larvae prey upon citrus mealy bugs and the related cottony cushion scale, red spiders, and Oriental fruit moth larvae, as well as the peculiar thrips, a tiny but often serious pest of citrus fruit, wheat, and many other cultivated cereals and flowers. Because

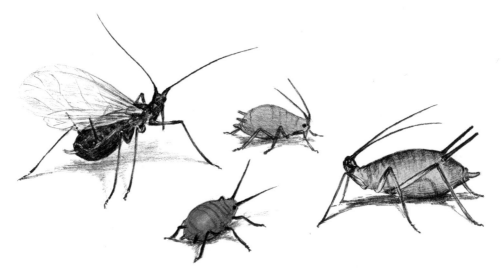

*Aphids, or plant lice. The larger individuals are females, the smaller ones nymphs. Wingless females give birth to living young without mating.*

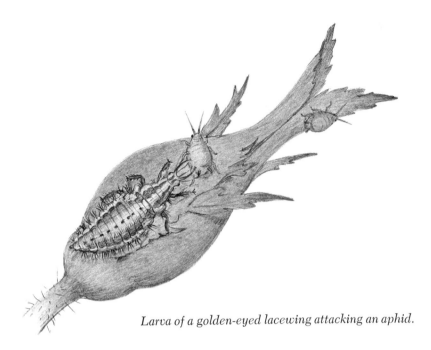

*Larva of a golden-eyed lacewing attacking an aphid.*

most of these small pest insects have tremendous reproductive powers and several generations usually occur during each season, it takes a great many hungry predators to keep them in check. Any small aphid-hunting insect is therefore a valuable ally in the attempt to control, biologically instead of chemically, these injurious members of the insect clan. "Aphid lions," as green lacewing larvae are popularly known, are small, unattractive, and less well-known than the lady beetles and their larvae, but they nevertheless perform the same valuable type of service.

Some species of lacewings have smooth-skinned larvae; those of many others, however, have warty skins covered with bristly hairs. The latter have evolved a peculiar trait: they cover themselves with the dry skins of their victims. These skins adhere to the hairs, which often end in small hooks, and soon form a kind of trash pile beneath which the larva all but disappears. This camouflage undoubtedly has

*Trash-covered larva of a green lacewing.*

some value while the larva remains motionless; the moment the tiny bit of fluffy debris starts to move about, however, the illusion is shattered. Even so, a predator attempting a bite may wind up with a mouthful of dry skins instead of a juicy larva.

Lacewings may breed several generations in a season. When cold weather comes, adults as well as larvae hibernate. The adults seek out cool but sheltered places and may be found in garages, greenhouses, and sheds. The immature insects spend the winter in a quiescent state, well protected in a cocoon that looks like a tiny globular barrel. It is usually tucked away snugly in a crevice under tree bark, or under debris between the roots of trees, or attached to the underside of a dead leaf. When the time comes in the spring for

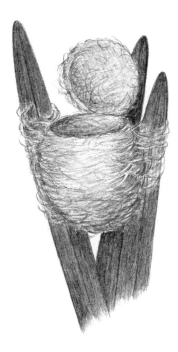

*Empty pupal cocoon of a green lacewing.*

the insect to leave the cocoon, the pupa, with special mandibles used only for this chore, snips through the silken threads until it has converted the top of the cocoon into a hinged lid that opens upward to let the pupa emerge. Only then does the pupal skin split to free the mature insect, which is now ready to begin its life as a winged adult.

Because lacewings, like most other nocturnal insects, are attracted by light, they will often be found clinging to door and window screens in the summer, and for the same reason will even sometimes find their way inside a house at night. Needless to say, these insects should never be killed. Instead, they should be picked up carefully and released (see the Appendix for methods of doing this), so that they can have a chance at starting new generations of beautiful and beneficial insects.

*Brown lacewing, enlarged about six times.*

Not so attractive as the green lacewing but every bit as beneficial is another closely related family of Neuropterons. These are the Hemerobiidae, or brown lacewings. Mostly much smaller than their green relatives—a common North American species measures only about half the size of a common green species—they are nevertheless efficient predators in their own right.

The adults, which have brown wings that frequently bear dark spots, in most cases do not exceed one quarter of an inch in length, although a few species are larger. Like the green lacewings, they are found in many different parts of the world, and often occur side by side with the former. In some regions, the brown lacewings are dominant.

The larvae, which are proportionately smaller than the aphid lions, are popularly called "aphid wolves." As the name implies, their smaller size does not mean that their appetite for aphids and similar insects is small. In contrast to the larvae of their green relatives, the brown lacewing larvae seem to prefer as their hunting grounds the foliage of trees instead of that of low vegetation.

While the development and habits of both groups are similar, they differ in some respects. So far as we know, the eggs of brown lacewings do not have any stalks at their tips; the female simply glues them, singly or in small groups, to tree bark or the surfaces of leaves. The larvae of all known species, although hairy, do not have the warty skins of many green lacewing species. They also do not camouflage themselves with debris in the manner of their larger relatives.

After a three-stage larval development, the larva spins a cocoon either inside a rolled-up leaf or in a small crevice in the bark of a tree. When the time comes, the pupa chews through the threads of the cocoon and emerges. Like the green lacewing pupa, the brown lacewing pupa has to crawl a short distance before the pupal skin splits and releases the winged adult.

Because they do not have the green lacewings' unpleasant odor, brown lacewings seem to be more beset by predators such as birds and bats. All the same, the nocturnal habits of the adults and the small size and unobtrusive coloring of the larvae fortunately insure the survival of numbers sufficient to propagate the species. However, lacewings, like other beneficial insects that prey upon plant pests, have suffered greatly from spraying with chemicals that were intended to kill only the pests but that turned out more injurious by far to a variety of organisms deserving of our protection. Anything at all that would tend to increase the numbers of lacewings would be in our own best interests.

Members of several small, related families are found in different parts of the world, including the tropics and even hot, arid regions. Some of them are minute, yet their larvae are very beneficial predators, feeding mainly, like the aphid lions and aphid wolves, on small, soft-bodied insects injurious to cultivated plants. The Neuroptera include so many valuable members, and are so singularly lacking in injurious species, that the order must be considered to be one of the most consistently beneficial groups in the entire insect class.

# Ladybird Beetles

"Ladybug, ladybug, fly away home,
 Your house is on fire, your children alone ..."

Reciting this incantation, a child then is supposed to hold up its finger and permit a captive ladybird to "fly away home." In this way, the little red beetle often escapes—as it has escaped, for a long time—the usual fate of being instantly and instinctively killed that most insects suffer at the hands of man.

In one form or another, children of many countries have been singing this verse for hundreds of years, for it is an old tradition, handed down from generation to generation. Settlers brought it from Europe to the New World; today, the original meaning of the words has been pretty much lost on both sides of the Atlantic. Actually, the verse probably refers to the custom, widespread in many parts of Europe in the past, of burning the vines of the hop plants after the harvest had been brought in. Doubtless people noticed numbers of the little red beetles on the vines in the hop fields. That they also knew them to be beneficial is evident not only from the content of the rhyme, which contains a friendly warning of danger, but also from the implication that the beetle is about to be released. In addition, the many popular names by which this insect is known in various countries indicate that people were aware that they were dealing with a friendly insect. In Russian and French, for example, *Bojia karovka* and *vache à Dieu* mean "God's little cow." The English variations of the name—ladybird, ladybug, lady beetle—are short forms of "beetle of Our Lady," reminding people, as does the German *Marienkaefer*, that the little red insect was dedicated to the Virgin as far back as the Middle Ages.

The nature of the ladybirds' beneficial activities—their insatiable appetite for sap-sucking destructive plant lice and similar small insect pests—has been known for a long time, and suggestions for employing these beetles for the benefit of man can be found at quite an early date. In a volume on insects acquired by one of my ancestors almost one hundred and twenty years ago, a detailed and excellent description of ladybirds, their habits and life cycle, is found along with some beautiful steel engravings depicting the insect in different stages of development. The most interesting part is a paragraph in which their collection and release among aphid-infested plants is strongly urged as an effective means to control these pests.

For persons skeptical of the ability of so small a predator to effectively keep in check large-scale plagues of plant-eating insects, the Case of the Australian Ladybug should be an eye-opener. It all began in California after the gold rush had died down, a little over a hundred years ago. At that time, a new kind of treasure was discovered in the Golden State—the enormous profits that could be made from oranges and other types of citrus fruit. Citrus growers quickly amassed fortunes with the produce of their orange groves. But then disaster struck, for a newly imported insect pest—the cottony cushion scale—gained a foothold on the Coast and soon spread so rapidly among the citrus trees that it threatened to wipe out the entire indus-

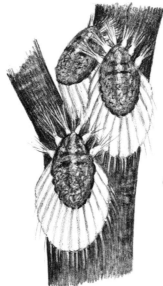

*Cottony-cushion scale insects.*

try. Trees died in large numbers, and those that survived were so badly crippled that they yielded hardly any fruit at all. By 1890, only twenty-two years after the tiny villain had been accidentally brought in from Australia, hundreds of thousands of trees had been killed. Every conceivable effort to fight back was tried without success. There seemed to be no help against these destructive insects.

In retrospect, it is difficult to tell what would have happened if Charles V. Riley had not held the office of chief entomologist of the United States Department of Agriculture at that time. For the citrus growers of California it was a piece of sheer good luck, for it is extremely doubtful that their industry would have survived without him. Born in London and educated on the Continent, Riley was a brilliant man, an artist and a naturalist especially interested in insects. Riley emigrated to the United States at the age of seventeen, and after working at various jobs was appointed state entomologist of Missouri at the age of twenty-five. Six years later, he moved up to his position in the federal Department of Agriculture. He had a quick and agile mind, great knowledge, and willingness to experiment with new ideas, such as large-scale efforts to fight pest insects by introducing, or even importing, their natural enemies. At the time, this seemed a fantastic undertaking to most people, for a hundred years ago popular knowledge about insects in this country was so scanty as to be almost nonexistent.

On hearing about the plight of the California citrus industry, Riley was struck by one peculiar fact. Even though the scale insect was wreaking such havoc among American trees, it appeared to be no problem at all in its native Australia. Some unknown factor seemed to act as a check upon the pest "down under." Riley shrewdly suspected that the something was another insect.

Acting upon this suspicion, Riley attempted to get funds from Congress to send a few men to Australia to investigate the situation. Congress was not willing to fund so outlandish a scheme, and Riley's request for money was refused. Not easily stopped, he tried a roundabout way to get what he wanted: he persuaded the Secretary of State to have two men sent to Australia on what was officially a mission that had nothing whatever to do with scale insects. Secretly, however, Riley instructed his two entomologists to look for possible parasites of the cottony cushion scale.

Almost immediately after arriving in Australia, one of them, a young man by the name of Albert Koebele, discovered a tiny fly whose eggs are laid on scale insects and whose grubs feed upon the pests. Koebele triumphantly sent a large batch of these flies to the United States, certain that he had found the solution of the problem. During his further studies, he also noticed a small red beetle devouring scale insects in large numbers, apparently preferring them to any other food. As an afterthought, Koebele decided to send along a few of these beetles.

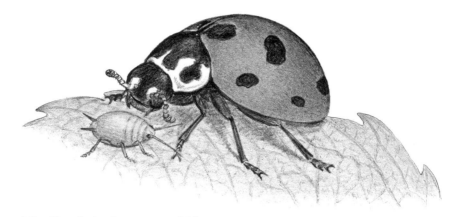

*Ladybird beetle feeding on an aphid.*

The parasitic flies, which were received with high hopes, proved a disappointment—something that frequently happens with imported insects that have to live away from their native conditions. In any case, the flies did not make a dent in the scale insect population. When the handful of ladybugs arrived, no one seriously considered the possibility that these few small beetles could succeed where thousands of flies had failed. However, the situation was so desperate that anything was given a try, and so the few specimens of *Rhodolia cardinalis,* as this species of ladybug is known to scientists, were placed on the infested trees. Several additional shipments arrived soon after, and so, in 1889, at the very height of the scale insect disaster, a grand total of some five hundred ladybugs were distributed in the orange groves of California.

The miracle no one had believed in any longer did happen. A scant two years later, the scale insects were completely under control throughout the state, and the cottony cushion scale has never again become a major problem.

Naturally, this amazing success was a great personal triumph for Riley and his concept of "biological control," and it offered clear proof that such programs can be successful. Since then, many different species of ladybirds have been drafted for pest-control duty by entomologists of various countries, and have been used with equally great success for the control of many different species of scale insects, mealy bugs, and aphids, all of which are closely related sap-sucking pests. Today there is hardly any country that has not imported and liberated some species of ladybirds, and in practically every single case these small aphid-killers have been successful in keeping the pests in check. The same species of Australian ladybug that saved California's citrus industry eighty years ago is today performing well in South Africa.

Lady birds are true beetles, members of the huge order Cole-

*Six different species of ladybirds.*

optera, or sheath-winged insects. Of the more than four thousand different species of ladybirds that make up the family Coccinellidae, practically all are beneficial, feeding upon aphids and similar pest insects during the larval as well as in the adult stage. Only a few species, members of a small group of plant-eating ladybugs, may become destructive to man's cultivated plants. One such American species is the Mexican bean beetle, which sometimes does considerable damage, especially in the southwestern parts of the United States. However, compared to the thousands of beneficial species, the few harmful kinds are really of no great importance and cannot detract from the overall value of this family.

The typical lady beetle is a small insect, usually only about one-

quarter to three-eighths of an inch long. It has a very characteristic shape, appearing almost circular when seen from above. The underside of the body is very flat; the upper surface is nearly hemispherical. The small head all but disappears below the first thoracic segment. Legs and antennae are short.

Coloring varies with the species; usually, however, some shade of red predominates. There are pink, orange, bright red, brick red, and maroon-colored lady beetles. In most cases, they have black spots, but a few are solid-colored, and still others are black with orange or red dots. The majority have some white or yellow markings on the otherwise black thoracic shield. The legs are black.

When disturbed, ladybugs often "play possum." They draw their legs flat against the body and remain motionless. A good defensive weapon is the evil-smelling yellow liquid they secrete from the joints of their legs when touched or handled. This secretion seems to be a fairly effective deterrent, for they apparently are rarely attacked by insect-eating animals such as birds.

After mating, the female seeks out a good spot for her offspring. This means a leaf that is infested with aphids, which will insure a plentiful food supply for the hatching larvae. The usually spindle-shaped eggs are attached to the plant surface either singly or in small groups. If the weather is warm, the first brood of many species in moderate climates may be almost fully grown by the end of May.

The hatchlings grow fast, for they have a voracious appetite and devour the various small, soft-bodied plant lice as fast as they can find them.

Lady beetle larvae are peculiar-looking creatures, with a flattened, long, oval body that in many cases exceeds that of the adult in length. There are considerable variations of coloring and appearance among the different species, with hues ranging from solid yellow or orange to slate gray or black with a yellow- or red-checkered pattern. The

*Ladybird larva attacking an aphid.*

skin may be smooth, hairy, or covered with spines. All these differences are literally only skin-deep; basically, the larvae all have the same habits. Like beasts of prey, they stalk about the flocks of aphids, slaughtering them at an incredibly fast rate. To many ants, in fact, they must seem to be exactly that: ferocious "tigers" attacking their cattle. Ants quite often treat aphids the way we treat our cows, and for the same reason. They guard and protect them because they want to milk them of their sweet secretions, sometimes even going so far as to transport them to better feeding ranges. In this way, ants on occasion indirectly damage many plants, among them plants valuable to man's economy.

A naturalist who observed several ladybug larvae throughout their development estimated that each of them ate more than three thousand scale insect larvae during the few weeks between the hatching of the egg and the forming of the pupa. This, of course, did not include the insects eaten by the adult. I once watched both an immature and an adult lady beetle of the kind that preys upon rose aphids, and recorded that the larva ate fourteen aphids in little more than an hour. The adult was not so voracious, and also seemed more choosy; in any case, it consumed only five aphids during the same time. All the same, if we multiply these figures by hundreds or thousands, it is easy to see why a sizable army of ladybugs is a most efficient pest control. Their importance is further enhanced by the fact that the female may lay many hundreds, and sometimes as many as a thousand, eggs in her lifetime, and that the short duration of the larval stage permits several generations per year. In this way, together with the aphid-eating larvae of a number of other insects, ladybugs are capable of checking even large-scale infestations of these destructive plant pests.

*A ladybug pupa.*

After completing its growth, the ladybird larva changes into a pupa, which glues the tip of its abdomen to the underside of a leaf or some similar surface. If a pupa is touched, it reacts to the disturbance with a hammering movement. Approximately a week or ten days later, the adult beetle emerges, seeks a mate, and the entire cycle is ready to begin all over again.

While many ladybugs hibernate individually, other species gather in large numbers and crowd together in some suitable crevice or under loose bark to spend the winter. This preference has become a source of income to people on whose property such aggregations of ladybugs are found. In California, for example, the beetles are collected every year and sold by the thousands to owners of citrus groves. The offspring of those beetles tend to return to the old locations in the fall, and in turn are collected and sold the following spring.

With rare unanimity, agriculture experts agree that the ladybird beetle is one of our most important six-legged allies. Unobtrusive but faithfully efficient, this small red insect friend deserves our full and unqualified protection.

# Parasitic Wasps

As a group, wasps are among the most disliked and feared of all insects because of their poison stings and their reputedly short tempers and aggressive natures. I always marvel at the widespread ignorance and misconceptions that prevail in regard to these insects. Most persons do not know that only a relatively few among the tens of thousands of species of wasps are likely to sting human beings, and that many do not even possess stings. Erroneous ideas about wasps stem chiefly from the widespread popular belief that all wasps are hornets or yellow jackets, live socially in paper nests, and are a (sometimes painful) nuisance to people hoping to enjoy picnics or barbecues, or to housewives canning fruit. As a matter of fact, the paper wasps, which include the above-mentioned hornets as well as a number of other species, are but one subdivision of a large group of highly diversified insects with a bewildering variety of habits, ways of life, and physical characteristics. Most of them never bother human beings and are satisfied to be left alone and go their own ways, and a great many are directly beneficial to man because they act as checks upon a large number of different plant-eating insects harmful to valuable plants.

Despite such facts, it is not always easy to convince people that their prejudice against wasps is largely unjustified. Distrust of insects in general, and stinging insects in particular, often enhanced by lingering memories of painful encounters with yellow jackets, are responsible for this widespread bias. I am always quite pleased if I can make even modest progress against such attitudes—for instance, when I convinced one of our neighbors that he was killing off his own good friends by destroying the nests of mud-dauber wasps, which provide their young with food consisting of various and frequently injurious insects. Now his mud daubers build their nests unmolested. And I was delighted when the young man who delivers our groceries displayed great interest in my explanation of why a wasp with a long "stinger" is not only quite harmless but actually highly beneficial. More general knowledge about insects as well as more specific knowledge about wasps is the best deterrent against indiscriminate killing, which more often than not eliminates useful predators.

The Hymenoptera, or membrane-winged insects, which include wasps, ants, and bees, are undoubtedly the most diversified of all the groups among insects. Members of this, the third-largest insect order, are found in every part of the world from the Arctic to the desert and the tropical rain forest. Many species, of which the honeybee is by far the best known, have developed complex societies and a high level of social organization. A few have degenerated into types of social parasitism that is often difficult to believe.

Hymenoptera vary in size from creatures so minute that you need a magnifying glass to see them to hefty individuals with a body length of several inches. They are distinguished by two pairs of wings, of which the hind pair is somewhat the smaller and in flight is joined to the forewings by a row of hooks. The wings are more or less transparent, although often tinted, mostly with browns and grays, but sometimes with bright colors. The first abdominal segment is joined to the thorax; in the majority of hymenopterous groups the following segment (or segments) is so constricted as to form the typical "wasp waist." The antennae are fairly long, and in many species have a pronounced bend, or "knee." In the advanced types, the ovipositor has been modified to form a sting. Especially among bees, a body covering of fine hairs forms a kind of fur that makes these insects look bigger than they really are.

Some Hymenoptera are among the best-known insects in the world. We have to think only of the ever-present ants and the proverbial busy bees. Since ancient times, honeybees have been an important part of man's economy, furnishing him with highly useful products such as beeswax and honey. Even more important were, and are to this day, their invaluable services as cross-pollinators. They fertilize many of man's most important plants, which otherwise could not produce seeds or fruit.

*Two hymenopterous insects: the bee, on the left, has a furry body-covering and pollen baskets on her legs. The wasp, on the right, has no fur, no pollen baskets, and a very pronounced "wasp waist".*

Scores of books have been written about honeybees. They most certainly are among man's best insect friends, but as this book features insects valuable to man because they are the natural enemies of other, plant-eating species, we will confine the remarks on bees to a few general observations. Bees evolved from wasps, with whom they have much in common. "Flower wasps," the old German name for bees, is in fact a good description. The chief difference between bees and wasps is that the former have become adapted to visiting flowers and to living exclusively, both in the larval and adult stages, upon pollen and nectar. The majority of wasps, on the other hand, are still predators. The adults usually enjoy sweet foods such as honey, sugar, and fruit juices, but most wasp larvae need a meat diet, and feed—or are fed by the adults—on other insects or insect relatives such as spiders. It is precisely the feeding habits of their larvae that make so many wasps valuable allies of man.

Only a relatively few among the countless wasp species are social, building community nests in which they raise their young. Many others are so-called solitary species, each of whose females builds her own nest and then provisions it with dead or paralyzed insects before laying her eggs in it. The earlier-mentioned mud dauber, as well as the potter wasp with its beautifully fashioned jarlike nests,

*A mud dauber wasp with a load of mud. This species has very long legs and a "wasp waist" consisting of a long thin stalk.*

belong to this group. The skill and persistence of these insects is often amazing. I observed one mud dauber female for days as she built her nest in the space between the screen and window of our bathroom. Having found a gap large enough to squeeze through where the screen meets the metal frame, she evidently felt this to be a safe place for her nest. Also, we had thoughtfully provided the material by having a load of topsoil delivered and piled up in the garden below, across from the bathroom window. The female would fashion a little bit of topsoil into a ball of mud and then fly up to the window at an uncannily accurate angle despite the downward pull of her heavy load. After the nest was finished, she provided each of the eleven individual "nurseries" with insects, and then plugged the openings. The eggs she laid were thus well provisioned, and most of the young successfully hatched, developed, and left the nest–eight open cells being mute evidence of that fact. Only three eggs for some reason failed to hatch. After taking down and opening the still-plugged cells later in the year, I found them stuffed with the dry bodies of insects, apparently some kind of small caterpillar.

The wasps we are mainly concerned with here because of their importance as pest controls do not go to so much trouble in caring for their young as the mud dauber described above. Known as parasitic wasps, they are considered somewhat more primitive. They include several families, each with a large number of different species.

Because the words "parasitic" and "parasite" will be used extensively in connection with these wasps, as well as with certain flies described in the following chapter, it is well to make sure that the terms are correctly understood as they apply to these insects. The typical parasite is any organism, plant or animal, that lives in any one of three different ways: in, on, or with another organism and obtains food, and usually shelter, at the host's expense. Especially the first two types, known respectively as endo- and ectoparasites, are dependent for their life and livelihood upon the host. If the host dies, they die too. It is thus not in the parasite's own best interest to kill its provider. Normally, therefore, parasites, unless they occur in abnormally large numbers, do not fatally injure the host organism.

In the case of the parasitic wasps, the situation is quite different. In reality, these insects are predators, but instead of killing their prey quickly, for the most part they kill it slowly, over a period of time varying from days to weeks, or even months. But they *always* kill it— a clear and important distinction between them and the true parasites. Because of this distinction, many entomologists prefer the term "parasitoid" as being more nearly correct in describing these insects. The suffix -*oid*, of course, always designates something that resembles, or is like, the word that precedes it. A spheroid, for example, is a sphere-like body. Even though today most entomologists use the terms "parasite" and "parasitic" when describing parasitoid insects, it is well to keep in mind that the latter are important as controls of injurious species precisely because they do not just parasitize, that is, live as parasites on the pests, but actually kill them.

In most cases, the parasitic wasps follow more or less the same pattern. It begins with the female seeking a suitable host insect, often a larva such as a caterpillar. She then deposits a single egg in the host with the help of her ovipositor. In this way, she has to parasitize quite a few insects before all her eggs have been laid. Inside the host, the larva hatches and begins to feed. At first, the vital organs of the victim are not attacked; instead, the wasp grub lives on fatty tissues and similar nonvital body parts. The host therefore can grow and develop and, if it is a caterpillar, in some cases even change into a pupa. Inside, however, the wasp larva also has grown and is nearing the end of its larval stage. At that point, it begins to feed on the host's vital organs, and finally emerges from what is left of the body of its victim, which in most cases is only the empty skin. Spinning a cocoon,

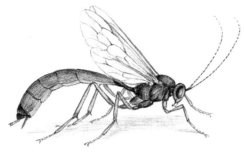

*A European species of ichneu-mon wasp that parasitizes the caterpillars of the pine moth, a serious pest of coniferous trees.*

the wasp grub pupates and after a while emerges as a winged adult.

Many parasitic wasps lay several eggs in a host if the latter is large enough to support a number of larvae–which the female seems to know instinctively. Another specialization is the development of many individual wasp larvae from a single egg, known as polyembryonic development. It is based upon the same principle as production of identical twins or triplets, found in many animals including man, but in these usually only as a rare occurrence. Naturally, all the adults developing from a single egg are of the same sex.

One of the largest and most beneficial of the parasitic wasp groups is the ichneumon wasp. The word "ichneumon" means "tracker" in Greek, and is another name for the mongoose, the renowned snake-killer of India.

Ichneumon wasps are at the same time the most primitive and the largest of the parasitic wasp groups. While the majority are small- to medium-sized insects, a few reach a length of several inches. Sometimes they are incorrectly referred to as ichneumon flies, even though their two pairs of wings place them clearly and unmistakably in the hymenopterous group.

In North America alone, there are many hundreds of different species of ichneumon wasps. Most of them are beneficial because they parasitize injurious insects, but some prey upon species that are them-selves beneficial. Although appearance varies considerably with the species, they all have certain basic features in common: They are slender insects with long, threadlike antennae; their elongated abdomen is either cylindrical or, in about half the species, sickle-shaped, and is vertically flattened as though it had been squeezed. Many females have long, thin ovipositors that may far exceed the length of the body. These wasps are often feared by persons who do not know what kind of insect they are, and who believe the ovipositor to be an especially powerful poison sting. In fact, however, the wasps are

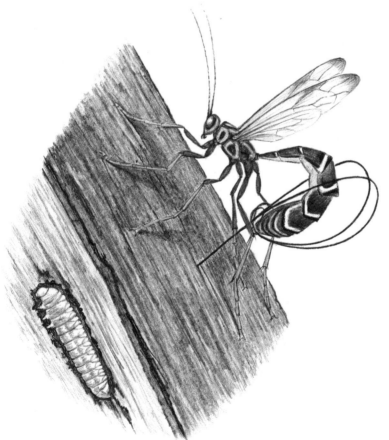

*The ichneumon wasp* Megarhyssa *drilling into the trunk of a tree with her long ovipositor. A portion of the wood has been removed in the illustration in order to show the horntail grub hidden in the heartwood of the tree.*

A *horntail, a primitive wood-boring relative of the wasps.*

dangerous only to the various host insects that they seek out and parasitize as food for their young.

Among the largest American ichneumon wasps are the species of the genus *Megarhyssa.* In some cases, the body of the these wasps may attain a length of almost two inches, not counting the female's ovipositor. If the latter is included, the over-all length is increased to almost five inches. With this long, thin ovipositor, the wasp can drill through several inches of wood and reach the tunnels of the horntail larvae, which bore into the heartwood of shade trees such as elms, maples, and beeches, greatly damaging the wood. Horntails are primitive, plant-eating relatives of the wasps belonging to the large group of sawflies.

The female ichneumon wasp has an uncanny instinct for locating horntail larvae beneath the wood or bark of a tree. She always drills the hole in a way that permits her ovipositor to reach the larva hidden below and deposit her egg on or near it.

Another ichneumon wasp, whose larval food preferences are even more beneficial to man, is a small insect, measuring not more than three-eighths of an inch in length. *Hyposoter pilosulus,* as it is known to entomologists ( common, or popular names, exist only for a minority of insect species), is an important parasite of a moth whose caterpillars are the notorious fall webworms. The medium-sized moths,

*The ichneumon wasp* Hyposoter pilosulus, *an important parasite of the fall webworm.*

which have a pure white and a spotted-color phase, lay their eggs especially on cherry and other fruit trees. When they occur in great numbers, their caterpillars are capable of completely defoliating the trees. The caterpillars live in communal groups inside a large silk web that they have spun and with which they envelop the branches of their food trees and are often confused with the even more obnoxious and injurious tent caterpillars. The latter, frequently found in huge numbers, also live in communal webs. However, distinguishing between the two is easy: fall webworms place their webs in the tips of branches, tent caterpillars in the forks or in the crotches of young trees. Both the tent caterpillar and the fall webworm are attacked by a number of parasitic wasps and flies, the ichneumon *Hyposoter* being one of the most important natural enemies of the webworm.

Several other parasitic wasp groups include valuable and effective controls of various pest insects. Prominent among these groups are the Braconid, Chalcid, and Trichogrammatid wasps. Most of these are small, and some are minute. One of the most valuable, from man's point of view, is the small (under a quarter of an inch long) Braconid *Apanteles glomeratus,* which selects as hosts such destructive pests as

*A pupa of the large white cabbage butterfly with the holes made by the emerging parasitic wasps.*

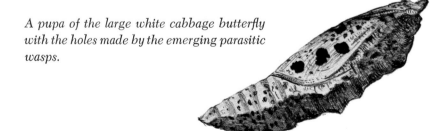

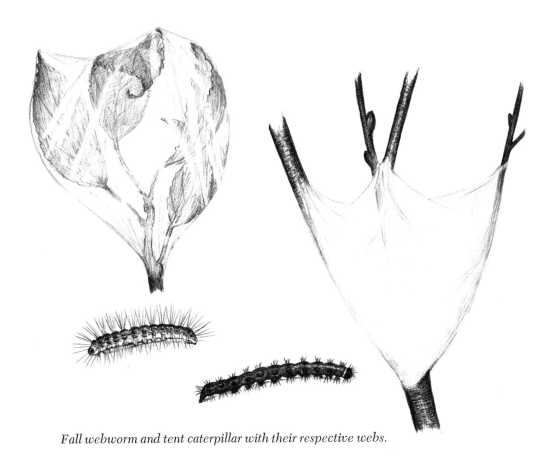

*Fall webworm and tent caterpillar with their respective webs.*

the tomato hornworm—actually the larva of a sphinx moth—and the caterpillar of the cabbage butterfly. This is one of the cases in which a female, sensing that the host is large enough to provide food for more than one wasp grub, lays a number of eggs in a single host. Dying caterpillars are sometimes covered with the tiny white cocoons –"caterpillar eggs" to persons with little knowledge of natural history —spun by the emerging *Apanteles* larvae.

Because the life cycle of many small parasitic wasps is relatively short, they can have several generations in a year, which of course increases their value as pest controls. A good example is another small Braconid, which attacks a number of different moth and butterfly larvae, among them the strawberry leaf roller and the Oriental fruit moth. The latter is a pest of peach trees, and a close relative of the codling moth, one of the most destructive insects known. *Macrocentrus ancylivorus*, the above-mentioned Braconid wasp, is especially useful because the female may lay as many as five hundred eggs in her lifetime, and larval development is completed within a period of about four weeks, making possible several generations per season. Attempts to use this wasp as effective control of pest species through large-scale rearing of larvae continue.

Many tiny wasps of both the Chalcid and the Trichogrammatid families are very valuable because they parasitize such ever-present plant pests as aphids, whose reproductive powers are so great that there is the constant danger of huge "population explosions" unless they are consistently kept in check. Because of that, there can never be too many natural enemies of aphids. Only the combined efforts of the various aphid-hunters can result in successful control.

The Trichogramma wasps are so minute that many can hardly be seen with the naked eye. Adults of one species, for example, measure only about one-fifth of a millimeter, which is about 1/120 of an inch.

*A tiny Braconid wasp depositing her egg in the body of an aphid.*

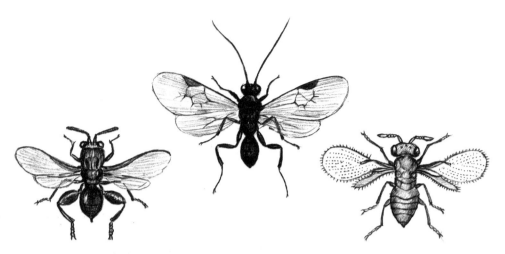

*Three small but important parasitic wasps that help control a variety of plant pests. The Trichogramma wasp on the right is less than 1/32 inch long.*

Because of their minute size, these wasps can be "egg parasites"— which means they deposit their eggs in the eggs of the host insect. Because they parasitize various moths and butterflies in this way, they are considered potentially highly effective controllers of certain destructive species. So far, attempts at large-scale rearing and releasing of these minute insects to control the codling moth have ended in failure, perhaps because at this time not all the pertinent facts about both host and parasite are known.

Other efforts, however, have been highly successful. In many parts of the world, a variety of pest insects have been effectively controlled by parasitic wasps. This includes such widely divergent regions as South Africa, Israel, and North America. In California, for example, the black scale insect, a major pest of citrus fruit, has been kept in check so successfully by an imported wasp parasite that over the years total savings directly traceable to the activities of this wasp have run into tens of millions of dollars. It seems clear, therefore, that in all future efforts at biological control of plant-eating insects, parasitic wasps will have an important part.

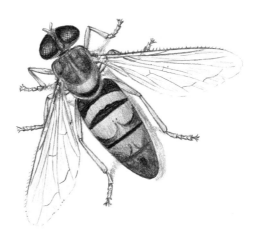

# Flower and Tachina Flies

The huge insect order of Diptera, or two-winged insects, which includes all flies and mosquitoes, contains a great many species harmful to man's cultivated crops, and quite a number that are directly dangerous to his health, as well as the health of his domesticated animals. We have only to think of the mosquitoes that spread yellow fever and malaria, and of the flies that act as carriers of sleeping sickness and other diseases. Relatively few persons, however, are aware of the fact that the common housefly, far from being just a nuisance, is the most dangerous of them all: a filthy creature on whose body surface up to half a million microorganisms have been found, and that has been established as the carrier of almost forty serious diseases, including typhoid and tuberculosis.

In view of these facts, it is not surprising that the word "fly" has become almost a synonym for a pestilential insect. This view goes back to ancient times: Beelzebub, the Hebrew word for Satan, means literally "Lord of Flies." Astute observers, despite their lack of factual scientific knowledge, the Hebrew people of long ago correctly associated flies with filth, decay, and decomposition. They were also painfully aware of the activities of the stinging and blood-sucking members of the group.

Considering the many entries on the debit side of Diptera's ledger, it is perhaps not surprising that even today, the credit side is often not properly acknowledged. With relatively few exceptions, entire families of flies are beneficial to man. Some are among his most valuable allies in the fight against various harmful insects. In this chapter we will take a look at the two most consistently beneficial of these groups, both of which play an important if generally unrecognized and unappreciated part in the control of certain common pest insects.

Of the two groups, the *Syrphidae,* also known as flower flies, is the larger, with its thousands of species one of the largest of all the dipterous families. A cosmopolitan group, these insects are found in many different parts of the world. In addition to counting among their numbers many extremely useful species, the majority of these flies are also very attractively patterned. Their popular name of flower flies can be traced to their habit of visiting blossoms to feed upon the nectar.

Anyone who has looked at a flower bed on a sunny summer's day has probably seen these flies in action, although chances are that he was not aware of what kind of insect he was seeing. Many of the larger Syrphid flies are excellent wasp mimics, and are often mistaken for the latter. In some cases, it may be just a general resemblance, consisting of little more than a pattern and coloration—usually black and yellow—that appear somewhat wasplike at a glance. In many instances, however, these flies have evolved into such close mimics of specific wasps or bees that it takes a close inspection by an expert to tell model and mimic apart. Thus, one species may mimic a honeybee, another a large hornet, and still another a furry bumblebee. Some buzz loudly when caught, thus further enhancing their similarity to

*A large flower fly.*

hymenopterous insects. Understandably, no amateur would wish to pick up one of these flies for fear of finding out the hard way whether he is indeed dealing with a harmless fly or with a wasp or bumblebee equipped with a powerful poison sting. Presumably, birds and other would-be attackers also hesitate, and it therefore seems reasonable to assume that these flies benefit to some extent from their resemblance to stinging insects.

Upon closer inspection, certain details will usually reveal whether you are dealing with a fly or with a wasp or bee. Most easily recognized is the difference in the appearance of the head. Syrphids, like the majority of flies, have small or minute antennae that are often hardly visible. In addition, they have large, bulbous eyes that all but meet in the center. The hymenopterous models of flower-fly mimics, on the other hand, have medium-sized to long antennae that are often clubbed, and their eyes never come close to meeting in the center of the head. It is true that the most important difference between wasps and flies is the single pair of wings that distinguishes the latter; wasps, like other Hymenoptera, have two pairs. However, when the wings are folded over the back, it is by no means always easy just by looking at the resting insect to determine whether the wings consist of one or two pairs. In any case, the amateur entomologist would be well advised to exercise caution when capturing alive any wasplike insect. For those interested in the study of this and other insects, information on methods of capture and observation is provided in the Appendix, (p. 77).

In flight, flower flies are easy to spot. Most species deserve their other popular name, hover flies. I have often watched them above a blossom, hanging as though suspended in mid-air. Their wings move so fast that the human eye is incapable of seeing them. One moment the fly is there, the next moment it is gone, only to reappear a few seconds later as suddenly as it vanished.

While the larger flower flies, which average a half inch or more, often have the colors and patterns of some wasp or bee model they mimic, many of the smaller species gleam with beautiful iridescent or metallic blue or green coloring. These attractive hues are not caused by any pigment or coloring matter, but rather by minute, submicroscopic structures in the insect's integument, or outer body covering. By selectively absorbing certain wave lengths of light and reflecting others, these structures are capable of producing beautiful, pure colors. Unfortunately, many of these colors disappear after death because shrinkage of the integument destroys the structural basis for these nonchemical, nonpigmental colors.

As mentioned before, most Syrphid flies are habitual flower visitors. Because of this, they are very valuable cross-pollinators, fertilizing many flowers by transferring pollen from one blossom to another. This is especially true of the hairy kinds, to whose "fur" pollen easily clings.

Even more important to man than the activities of the adults, however, are those of some flower flies in their immature stages. We can roughly divide the flower-fly larvae into three groups according to their economic importance: those whose habits are harmful, indifferent, or beneficial to man. Because the last-mentioned is not only a very large group, but also the one in which we are chiefly interested here, we shall leave it for a later, detailed discussion, and first take a look at the other two.

The harmful species can be dealt with quickly, because they are a minority. Most important among them are the so-called bulb flies, whose larvae live in the bulbs and root stocks of flowers such as hyacinth, narcissus, and iris, often destroying the roots and causing damage for commercial planters and gardeners. An example of this type of Syrphid is the narcissus bulb fly, which originally came from Europe and was introduced into the United States and Canada in bulbs imported from Holland. Although the fly is now established in Canada and in scattered regions of the United States, it is not a problem of major proportions.

Roughly about one half of the flower flies are neither directly beneficial nor harmful to man. Most of these "indifferent" species spend their larval stages more or less in the conventional manner of fly grubs. They burrow in, and feed upon, decaying plant material and humus, and are mainly harmless–or most likely even useful–scavengers. Certain species are adapted for living in highly polluted waters, including actual sewage, as well as in decaying organic matter. The larva of the abundant bee-like drone fly, for example, has evolved an apparatus that permits it to live in the seepage from stables and other kinds of putrescence. The posterior end of the larva's body is so elongated as to form a slender tube that somewhat resembles the tail of a rat or a mouse. At the very tip of this tube is located the last of the many pairs of spiracles, or breathing holes, with which all insects are equipped. In order to get the air it needs while feeding in the polluted water below, the drone fly larva simply keeps the tip of its "tail" with the breathing holes above the surface. Entomologist Alexander B. Klots called this apparatus the forerunner of the modern diver's snorkel tube.

*A drone fly. Often mistaken for a bee, this fly gave rise to the ancient legend that bees generate spontaneously from rotting carcasses.*

Because of its peculiar appearance, the grub is often called "rat-tailed maggot." It is also known as "little mouse" in certain regions of Europe. Despite its unappetizing choice of environment as a larva, the adult drone fly, which closely resembles a honeybee, is as consistent a flower visitor as are most of its relatives.

The fly's resemblance to a honeybee is responsible for an ancient myth. It originated about two thousand years ago and was first recorded by Ovid, the Roman poet and writer. This myth was firmly believed until relatively modern times and deals with the formula for creating large swarms of bees. All one had to do, according to the story, was to kill an ox and leave its carcass to decompose. Upon returning to the remains after a period of time, one would be astonished to see a large number of bees swarming around. Miraculously, the rotting flesh had generated the bees!

If anyone had bothered to investigate this story a little more closely, he would have observed not only the female drone flies depositing their eggs on the carrion but also the maggots developing and finally turning into the beelike adults. This type of nature observation, however, is a relatively recent development. In the Middle Ages, few would have bothered, certainly not if an explanation of a phenomenon had already been established by an ancient authority.

The flower flies with which we are most concerned in this book are not the scavengers but the predators. They are the ones that, by their feeding habits, directly and often importantly benefit man. This is true of perhaps as many as half the members of the family, whose grubs are small but voracious predators and fortunately have an insatiable appetite, particularly for aphids and other soft-bodied insect pests. Despite the fact that the tiny predators, many of which measure less than one-quarter of an inch in length, have neither legs nor eyes, and also do not possess biting or chewing mouth parts, they manage to slaughter aphids in large numbers. Crawling about on

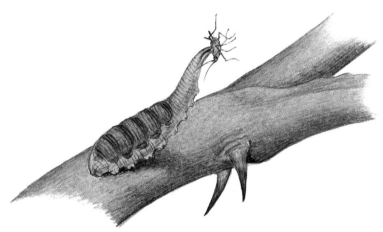

*Having captured an aphid, a flower-fly larva
lifts it into the air to drain its juices.*

infested vegetation, they pierce their victims' soft bodies with their mouth hooks, and suck the body juices until nothing is left but the empty skin. In many cases, the grub will lift the aphid high into the air while draining it of its juices, very much in the manner of a person tilting a bottle from which he is drinking in order to empty its contents.

In contrast to those pale-looking fly grubs that live hidden away from sight, the predatory flower-fly larvae that spend their days out in the open hunting on plants are often brightly colored. Many have green and brown tints that offer them maximum camouflage as they seek out their victims and that help protect them from other, larger predators. For this we can be grateful, for flower-fly larvae are among our most valued allies in the never-ending battle to control insect pests.

An excellent example of what these larvae can accomplish occurred years ago on Long Island, when the entire potato crop was threatened by an infestation of aphids. The situation appeared quite hopeless until the Syrphid flies went to work. Checkmating the tremendous reproductive capacities of the aphids through their own considerable reproductive powers and the voracious appetite of their larvae, the flower flies were largely responsible for saving the potato crop in this case. People living in that part of Long Island, however, complained about the large number of "wasps" that were flying around that year. Little did they realize that their complaints were singularly unjusti-

*A common species of Tachina fly.*

fied in view of the fact that these wasplike insects were the adult flower flies whose larvae were busily engaged in saving the potato crop.

While Syrphid flies concentrate their attacks on the smallest of the plant-feeding insects, the *Tachinidae,* or Tachina flies, employ a different method for bringing larger types of injurious insects under control. These flies are parasitic, or, rather, parasitoid, with habits very similar to those of the parasitic wasps discussed in the preceding chapter.

Some Tachina flies are rather indiscriminate, attacking a variety of insects including grasshoppers, caterpillars, beetles, and sawflies, the primitive relatives of wasps. Some are specialized and confine themselves to a few related species. This latter habit makes certain Tachina flies perfect controls for selected insect pests. An example are two European species of Tachinids imported in attempts to control two of the most destructive moths in the United States: the browntail and gypsy moths. The latter is even today a serious pest, and outbreaks of infestations that defoliate shade trees in New England are regularly reported. The browntail, which belongs to the same group, also used to be a serious pest. However, the imported Tachina flies successfully brought that moth under control, and it has not been much of a problem since. The flies have not done so well with the gypsy moth, but experiments are continuing and hopefully will one day be crowned with the same success as was the case of the browntail.

Tachina flies are found all over the world. They vary a good deal in size and appearance. Most typically, they are very hairy or bristly, and usually have somber dark gray or black coloring Many are about the size and color of a housefly. Some, however, are much smaller, and others considerably larger, and a few have very attractive bright colors, including yellow and orange as well as metallic blues and greens.

*Tachina fly ready to lay its eggs on a handsome but destructive gypsy moth caterpillar.*

The majority of female Tachina flies launch a new generation by first selecting a suitable host insect and then fastening their eggs to the skin of the victim. In many species, the white, oval-shaped eggs are quite flat. The females of some species go a step further and actually insert an egg into the body of the host, while others, much less painstaking, simply deposit their eggs on the host's food plant, and leave to the larvae the job of finding their own way to a suitable victim. In most instances, but not always, only a single larva will develop inside any one host insect. In those cases where the victim—most often a caterpillar—hibernates in the larval stage, the Tachina grub also spends the winter in a quiescent stage inside the host, resuming its deadly work only in the following spring. A great many of these grubs almost completely devour the host insect before they finally pupate, leaving behind nothing of their victim's body except perhaps a few hard, chitinous parts such as the head.

Many adult Tachina flies commonly visit flowers and, because of their bristly hairs, they are good cross-pollinators, thus adding another beneficial activity to those of their larvae. A "housefly" sitting on a blossom is most likely not a housefly at all, for these insects are not often attracted by flowers. Very possibly, the rather unattractive gray or black fly is a Tachina fly enjoying a sip of nectar. The smaller species of these flies are seen less often, because they lead a rather secretive life among the grasses and bushes where they find the right host insects for their offspring.

The total debt we owe to both the Syrphid and Tachinid flies cannot be accurately estimated because statistics are lacking; we know with certainty only that it is tremendous. The same holds true for our other insect allies, some of which, as we have seen in this book, have saved entire agricultural enterprises and with them the livelihoods of countless persons. As a measure of our gratitude, and in our own best interests, we should explore every possibility of employing these biological controls on a wider scale, instead of killing them off, along with their victims, with our pernicious poison sprays. As Alfred Brehm, a nineteenth-century naturalist, put it almost a hundred years ago: "These are the tiny but safe guardians which Nature provided in order to counteract any upsetting of the balance of her incredibly complex interrelated household." Once we use every possible means to act according to this insight, we will have made a giant step towards restoring, at least in part, the delicate balance of nature, which we have all but destroyed through our lack of wisdom and foresight.

# Appendix

# Guide to Observing Insects
# in Your Back Yard

Have you ever thought of a magnifying glass as being a free ticket to some fascinating nature shows, with a front seat guaranteed every time you use it? Chances are you will be surprised at how a seemingly lifeless plant can turn into a jungle teeming with a variety of strange creatures. Best of all, this activity can be found in your own or your friend's back yard or garden; in a corner of a meadow or a park near your home; or, in fact, almost anyplace where there is a patch of vegetation, even if it happens to be only weeds.

If you are lucky enough to have your own back yard, yours is a field for study involving representatives of probably all the insect groups discussed in this book, plus many, many more. If you think this is an exaggeration, consider the story of Frank E. Lutz, a former head of the Entomological Department of the American Museum of Natural History in New York. He once mentioned to a friend that he believed the average back yard would yield about a thousand different species of insects. "That's a lot of insects," said the friend, doubtfully shaking his head. Taking up the challenge, Dr. Lutz set out to prove his point—and, to his own surprise, ended up with almost fifteen hundred species. Naturally, he wrote a book about this venture; naturally, the title was *A Lot of Insects.*

I want to make clear that I am not about to discuss the collecting and killing of insects. That is a different and separate subject; should you be interested in starting a collection, you will find help and advice in your local Natural History museums. There are also many books on the subject from which you can learn the basic requirements.

In this book, however, we are concerned only with live insects, and with keeping them alive, especially the beneficial species already discussed. You will learn all sorts of interesting facts about these insects by observing and studying them. In addition, the knowledge you acquire will contribute to their protection and preservation, because you can pass on information to others and thus help prevent the inadvertent killing of our insect allies.

Because so many of these insects are very small, a magnifying glass is absolutely necessary for observing detail. Even a magnification of three or four times will reveal details you would never suspect by looking at these creatures with the naked eye. While much can be observed outdoors on the spot ("in the field," as scientists call it), there are often times when you will want to get a closer look at the objects of your study. At such times, capturing them alive and observing them at leisure is the obvious solution. This presents no difficulty at all if the insects in question are flightless—grubs and other larvae, for example—or even beetles such as ladybugs that are usually slow to fly and can easily be observed, often together with their larvae, by gathering an aphid-infested twig or flower, putting it in a vase, and then looking at it under a magnifying glass. What you will then see are fat, placid aphid "cows" and their small "calves," all tightly packed together and busily sucking the plant's vital juices, or slowly moving around in a search for better feeding places. Suddenly, along comes one of the black-and-orange, six-legged "tigers," otherwise known as ladybug larvae, and grabs one of the fat aphid cows. On the other side of the stem, perhaps, an adult ladybug has just snatched another aphid from the edge of the herd. Or you may witness a peculiar, wormlike green or brown-and-white creature pick up an aphid and lift it high into the air. As you watch, the aphid's body gets thinner and thinner, the futile struggling of its legs slows down as the flower-fly larva drains its victim's vital juices. Finally, only the skin and legs remain and are cast aside.

I have often been able to witness all the dramas described above just by walking around the corner of the house, selecting a flower or branch with aphids on it, and then settling down with a magnifying glass to watch. Things really get exciting when ant "cowboys" are around to protect their aphid herds against the various predators.

Observing flying insects is another matter, for the simple reason that most of them will fly away if you come too close. Dragonflies can be watched from a distance because they are large enough for their detail to be distinguished, and, for the same reason, some of the larger ichneumon wasps are good subjects for study in the field. Any wasp is a rewarding subject for observation, regardless of whether it is building a nest or provisioning its young with food.

In order to study body detail and movements in small flying insects, you will have to capture them alive and unharmed. This is not always easy, but there are ways to do it without much equipment. At the end of this chapter, you will find a list of the insects discussed in this book and the capture method I have found to be effective in each case.

A good aid for capturing flower-visiting species is a clear plastic tumbler, or a water glass. First, wait until the insect is busily engaged in feeding on nectar or pollen, then cup the glass over the blossom it is sitting on. Then, as the insect instinctively flies upward, lift the glass from the flower just enough to permit sealing off the open bottom by pushing a piece of cardboard under the rim. You can now place the tumbler on a table and observe the insect as soon as it has calmed down. A good way to induce your captive to sit quietly is to feed it. In most cases, this is done by tilting the glass just enough to insert a drop of water mixed with honey or sugar. Sooner or later, nectar-feeding insects will find and drink from the droplet. Even those that do not eat nectar usually like moisture. Ladybugs and lacewings will readily drink from a drop of water and do not seem to mind at all if it is sweet.

In order to study detail more closely without the inconvenience of having to hold a magnifying glass, I invented an observation cage that is easy both to make and to use. You need a clear plastic tumbler, preferably of a plastic that is soft enough to be cut easily, and a circular magnifying glass with a diameter of about three inches, of the type used by stamp collectors.

cut here

First, find out the distance at which you have to hold the magnifying glass from the object in order to get the best focus. Then measure this distance from the rim along the side of the tumbler. Cut the bottom part of the tumbler away, so that you now have a plastic tube that is open at both ends. Place the magnifying glass over one of the open ends, choosing the one that fits better. Fasten the glass to the tumbler either with cloth or paper tape. This simple procedure gives you a transparent cage whose top is a magnifying glass, and which will permit you to study details of insects inside, especially if you can induce them to sit quietly while they accept food or water. In this way, you may be able to get a close look at a number of the insects listed below.[*]

Dragonflies       Practically impossible to capture without a net, and difficult to capture even with it. Persons without experience are likely to damage these insects and should be content to observe them in the field.

[*]These illustrations show the insects life size with the exception of the dragonfly, which is somewhat reduced.

Lacewings

Green lacewings are easy to capture. They are found on window and door screens in the summer, usually at night. They can be picked up by carefully clamping the outer tips of their wings between thumb and forefinger. Because the wings extend far beyond the body, the insect is not hurt when picked up in this way. For those who have doubts about this method, a glass or tumbler can be used.

Ladybugs

Easy to pick up without hurting them by moistening the tip of a finger and gently pressing it against the beetle's back. The ladybug will stick to the little bit of moisture long enough for you to transfer it to the observation cage.

Wasps

Caution should be observed with all types of wasps and wasplike insects, especially for those who have had little experience and cannot identify the various types. Wasps visiting flowers can be captured with the help of a tumbler, but for the inexperienced, only observation in the field is recommended.

Flies

Both Tachina and flower flies are consistent flower visitors. They are excellent, fast, and agile fliers, and not easily captured. However, a tumbler can be used if care is exercised not to throw a shadow or make a hasty movement.

Keeping notes on the types of insects that visit your back yard is an excellent idea. You may be able to identify quite a few species from the illustrations in this book, and many more with the help of one of the several good insect guides. Those you cannot identify can still be described as to size, color, pattern, etc., plus general identification such as "beetle," "fly," and so on. Such records, besides being interesting, are useful and provide information on local insect populations. For some of you, these records may very well be the beginning of a life-long interest in the diminutive world that plays so important a part in shaping our natural environment.

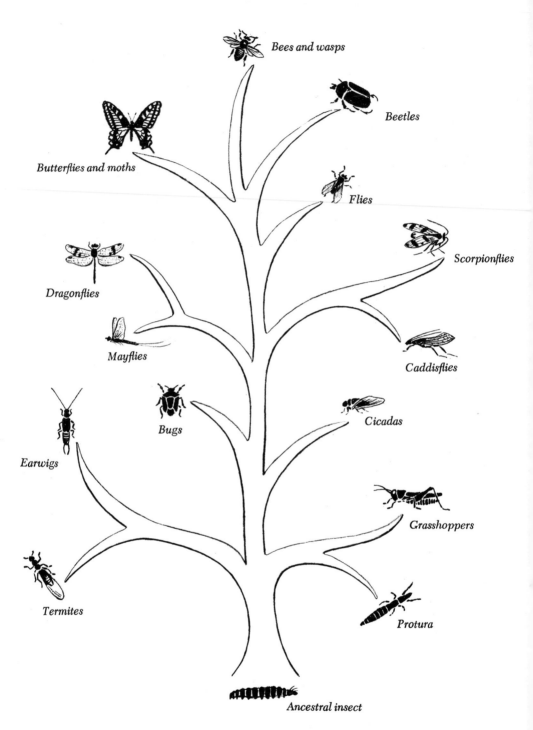

Bees and wasps

Beetles

Butterflies and moths

Flies

Scorpionflies

Dragonflies

Mayflies

Caddisflies

Earwigs

Bugs

Cicadas

Grasshoppers

Termites

Protura

Ancestral insect

Ancestral tree of the insects, starting with the most primitive and branching out into the more advanced members.

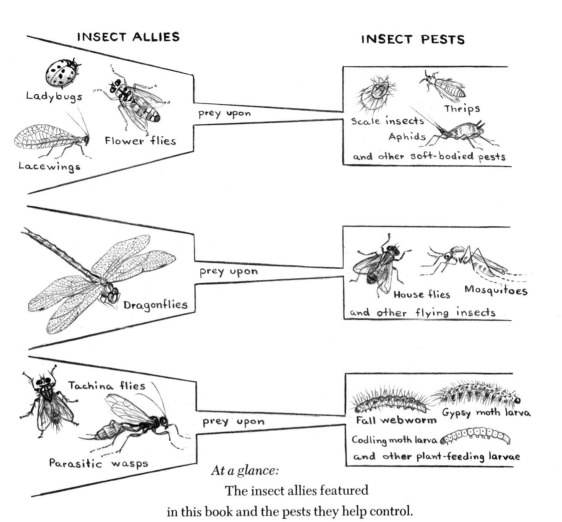

INSECT ALLIES

INSECT PESTS

Ladybugs

Flower flies

Lacewings

prey upon

Scale insects
Thrips
Aphids
and other soft-bodied pests

Dragonflies

prey upon

House flies
Mosquitoes
and other flying insects

Tachina flies

Parasitic wasps

prey upon

Fall webworm
Gypsy moth larva
Codling moth larva
and other plant-feeding larvae

*At a glance:*

The insect allies featured
in this book and the pests they help control.

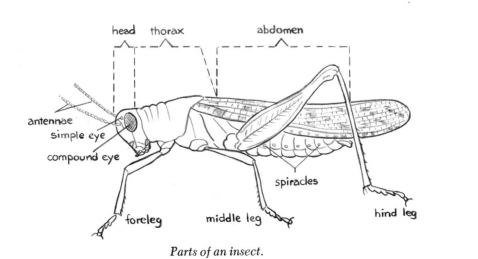

head   thorax   abdomen

antennae
simple eye
compound eye

spiracles

foreleg   middle leg   hind leg

*Parts of an insect.*

## DIRECT DEVELOPMENT *(silverfish)*

egg                   young                     adult

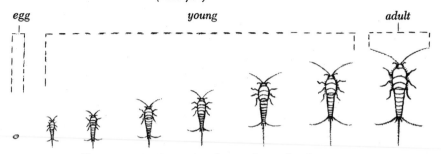

*The most primitive insects have a direct development. The young resemble the adults in all details.*

## GRADUAL DEVELOPMENT *(bug)*

egg                 nymphs                  adult

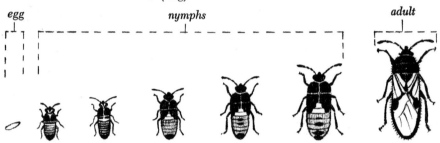

*The "gradual" development, or incomplete metamorphosis, is found in the more advanced insects. The young, called nymphs, lack certain adult features — functional wings, for example.*

## COMPLEX DEVELOPMENT *(butterfly)*

egg             larvae                pupa         adult

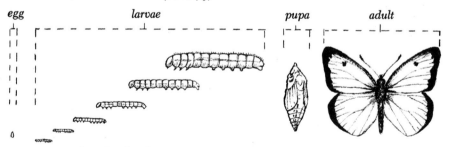

*Complex development, or complete metamorphosis, is a feature of the most advanced insects. It involves four stages: egg, larva, pupa, and adult. The immature young do not resemble the adults.*

*Various forms of development among insects.*

# Glossary

ab-do′men

The posterior section of the body, behind the thorax, in insects and crustaceans. The abdomen is made up of segments. The number of segments depends on the species, but no insect has more than eleven abdominal segments even in the immature stage, and fewer in the adult.

ad-vanced′

In zoology, a term used for animal groups whose anatomical structure, development, or both, have become more complex than that of their *primitive* relatives.

an-ten′nae (sing.: an-ten′na)

Movable, segmented organs of sensation on the heads of insects and certain other animals, including crustaceans. Popularly called *feelers* or *horns*.

ar-cha′ic

Going back to an earlier, more primitive time; said of anatomical features or types of development that, according to earliest fossil evidence, have persisted without evolutionary change.

bio-log′i-cal con-trol′

The method of employing various natural, non-chemical means, including other insects, in an effort to limit populations of noxious insects and thereby reduce or eliminate damage to valuable plants and animals.

cam′ou-flage

In zoology, body pattern and coloring of an animal that tend to let the animal blend in with the background and thus hide it from enemy eyes; a deceptive disguise that makes an animal inconspicuous.

| | |
|---|---|
| class | A comprehensive group of animals. In zoological classification, a class ranks above (is more complex than and contains) an order. Thus, mammals, birds, and insects are examples of animal classes. Each *class* has a varying number of *orders*, which are subdivided into *families*. Families, in turn, are made up of several *genera* (sing.: *genus*), and the *genera* are made up usually of a number of *species*. |
| co-coon′ | The envelope, often made of silk, that the larvae of many insects form about themselves as they pass into the pupal stage. The pupa remains in the cocoon until the adult insect emerges. |
| com′pound eye | The many-faceted, composite eye of an insect. |
| e-col′o-gy | That field of biology dealing with the interrelationship between organisms and environment. |
| en-to-mol′o-gist | A zoologist specializing in the study of insects. |
| fam′i-ly | A group of related animals forming a category that is above the *genus* and below the *order*. All the scientific names of families end in *-idae*, as in *Tachinidae*, the Tachina flies. |
| fos′sil | An impression or trace, such as a bone, of an animal or plant of a past geological age, which has been preserved in the crust of the earth. |
| ge′nus | A group of related species; in classification, a category ranking between the *species* and the *family*. The genus name is the first part of an animal's scientific name and is always capitalized and italicized, as in *Hyposoter pilosulus*. |
| grub | A rather stout, wormlike insect larva. |
| hi′ber-nate | To pass the winter in a lethargic state in which all activity is either much reduced or stopped altogether, and little or no food is consumed. |

lar′va | The immature, wingless, and often wormlike form, the second stage of *complete metamorphosis*, in which the young of *advanced insects* remain until time comes to pupate. The larvae of various insect species may be known as *grubs*, *maggots*, or *caterpillars*.

man′di-ble | In insects and certain other animals, the anterior mouth appendage that often forms biting jaws.

mem′brane | A thin, pliable, often translucent sheet or layer of animal or plant tissue.

met-a-mor′pho-sis | A marked and usually rather abrupt change in form and structure of an animal, most often accompanied by a change in way of life, food, etc.

mim′ic-ry | In the strict zoological sense, a superficial resemblance of certain animals, especially insects, to other, often unrelated, species, through which the *mimic* gains some protection.

mod′el | An animal, usually an insect, naturally protected either through weapons such as poison stings, or through distasteful or poisonous body juices, and which is *mimicked* by an unprotected species.

molt | To shed or cast off hair, feathers, outer layers of skin, etc., at certain times when the castoff parts are replaced with new growth. Among insects, only the immature young molt, never the adults.

nymph | The young of more primitive insects with *incomplete metamorphosis*. Nymphs of some insects resemble the adult; others do not at all. In both cases, however, they change into the adult form without any intermediate, pupal stage.

or′der | A category below a *class* and above a *family*.

o′vi-pos′i-tor | A specialized organ, found in many female insects, for depositing eggs.

par′a-site       Any plant or animal living on, in, or with another organism, called the *host*, at whose expense it gets food, shelter, and other advantages.

par′a-si-toid     An animal behaving in a manner similar to that of a parasite.

pest             A destructive or noxious animal, usually an insect. Pest insects are most often characterized by their ability to build up huge populations.

pred′a-tor       An animal that lives by preying upon others. Thus, both the lion and the praying mantis are *predatory* animals, even though one is a mammal and the other an insect.

prim′i-tive      Ancient, not highly evolved; said of groups resembling early ancestral types.

pro-tho′rax      The anterior segment of an insect's thorax.

pu′pa            The third stage of complete metamorphosis; an intermediate and usually quiescent form found in *advanced* insects.

spe′cies         The basic category of classification; a group of
(sing. and pl.)  animals, below a *genus*, that possess one or more distinctive characteristics in common, and that can and do interbreed and reproduce their distinctive features in their offspring. The second portion of an animal's scientific name, always spelled in lower case and italicized, is the species name, as in *Hyposoter pilosulus*.

scav′eng-er      An animal that lives on dead or decaying organic matter such as carrion, refuse, etc.

spi′ra-cle       A breathing hole; an external opening of the air tubes, or trachea, in insects and terrestrial arthropods, placed along the sides of the thorax and abdomen.

tho′rax          The middle section of an insect's body, bearing a pair of legs on each of its three segments.

# Index

Abdomen, definition of, 89
Advanced, definition of, 89
Antennae, definition of, 89
*Apanteles glomeratus,* 60-61
Aphids, 32, 44, 46-48, 80, 87;
    *ill.,* 32, 87
  cabbage, 32
  cotton, 32
  pea, 32
Aphid lions, 32, 37
Aphid wolves, 36, 37
Archaic, definition of, 89

Balance of nature, 15, 75
Beelzebub, 65
Bees, 52-53, *ill.* 53
Beetle of Our Lady, 40
Beetles, 45
  ladybird, 39-49, 84;
    *(see also* Ladybird beetles)
  Mexican bean, 45
Biological control, 14
  definition of, 89
*Bojia karovka,* 40
Browntail moth, 73

Calvert, Philip P., 26
Caterpillars, 60-63, 73
  cabbage butterfly, 61
  fall webworm, 59-60; *ill.,* 61
  gypsy moth, 73
  tent caterpillar, 59-60; *ill.,* 61
  tomato hornworm, 61

Chemical pest control, 11-12
  danger of, 12
*Chrysopidae,* 29
*Coccinellidae,* 45
Codling moth, 61, 63
Coleoptera, 45
Class, definition of, 90
Cocoon, definition of, 90
  lacewing, 34
  wasp, 56
Compound eye, 21; *ill.,* 87
  definition of, 90
Conservation, importance of,
  12-13
Cottony cushion scale;
    (*see also* Scale insects)

Damselflies, 20; *ill.,* 24
Dragonflies, 17-27, 83;
  *ill.,* 16, 17, 21, 83
  ancient, 20
  in art and folklore, 18
  eye, 21-22; *ill.,* 22
  flight apparatus, 20-21
  larvae, 19-20, 23, 27; *ill.,* 25
    capture mask, 24-25; *ill.,* 26
    gills, 25
    prey, 22
  legs, 22; *ill.,* 22
  mating, 23
  migrations, 20
  mouth parts, 22; *ill.,* 23
  nymph; *see* Larva